The Cathars: The History and Legacy of the Gnostic Christian Sect During
the Middle Ages
By Charles River Editors

The Occitan Cross, a Cathar symbol

About Charles River Editors

Charles River Editors is a boutique digital publishing company, specializing in bringing history back to life with educational and engaging books on a wide range of topics. Keep up to date with our new and free offerings with this 5 second sign up on our weekly mailing list, and visit Our Kindle Author Page to see other recently published Kindle titles.

We make these books for you and always want to know our readers' opinions, so we encourage you to leave reviews and look forward to publishing new and exciting titles each week.

Introduction

A medieval depiction of Cathars being expelled from Carcassonne in 1209

The Cathars

"The Roman Church...[says] that the heretics they persecute are the church of wolves. But this is absurd, for the wolves have always pursued and killed the sheep, and today it would have to be the other way around for the sheep to be so mad as to bite, pursue, and kill the wolves, and for the wolves to be so patient as to let the sheep devour them!" – Excerpt from the alleged writings of the Cathars

The unique, copper-red hue of the naturally cracked earth on the foothills of the French Pyrenees is obviously stunning, but if the rumors are to be believed, they, too, are rich with medicinal properties. For centuries, locals have been scooping up and bottling the precious dirt and turning them into an array of poultices, salves, and even tonics.

This land is also home to several legends and local traditions. When the earth is drenched by heavy storms, the crumbling red soil drifts into the River Aude, staining the water with crimson. This beautiful, yet haunting phenomenon, which the locals call the "blood of the Cathars," is a symbolic reminder of the blood shed by these "heretics" at the hands of the Catholic Church.

Despite the controversial events, and their supposed heresy, it seemed that the fall of the Cathars brought an everlasting curse upon the region. As one unnamed farmer, documented by French medievalist Jean Duernoy, put it, "Since the heretics were chased away from Sabartes, there is no longer good weather in this area." Another notary from Tarn echoed his sentiments, asserting, "When the heretics lived in these lands, we did not have so many storms and lightning.

Now that we are with Franciscans and Dominicans, the lightning strikes more frequently..."

But who were these Cathars, and why was the Catholic Church so committed to getting rid of them? *The Cathars: The History and Legacy of the Gnostic Christian Sect During the Middle Ages* examines the origins of the cult, their fascinating belief system, their gradual development over the years, and the events that contributed to their epic downfall. Along with pictures depicting important people, places, and events, you will learn about the Cathars like never before.

Genesis

"We must no more ask whether the soul and body are one than ask whether the wax and the figure impressed on it are one." – attributed to Aristotle

Nestled within an evergreen grove blanketing the crest of a hill 4,000 feet above the Montségur village stood its namesake – a strapping, sandy-beige fortress guarded by imposing walls and capped with a melange of gable and conical roofs. From below, there was little one could see of the colossal castle, or as the locals called it, the Château de Montségur, perched upon the round boulder of a hill. Not only was it half-hidden by the hill's natural formations, what was visible blended in with the naked rock, so that it appeared no more than a distinctive stone protuberance jutting out of its pinnacle. But if one were to lean against the parapet in the highest point of the castle, one would be treated to a panoramic view of the lush valleys and countryside of the Ariège, along the Pyrenees, the Montagne Noire (Black Mountain), and even parts of Toulouse.

M. Danis' aerial picture of the Château de Montségur

The courtyard

It was a particularly pitch-black evening on the 16th of March, 1244. The dainty breeze of the approaching spring caressed the mossy walls of the castle. The vibrant wildflowers surrounding the structure swayed slightly with the wind, but otherwise resembled static fireflies hovering above the grass. This scene would have been pretty as a picture had it not been for the discordance of tumbling targets, whizzing projectiles, and other telltale signs of a siege in the distance. Critters usually seen scurrying about freely were cowering in their burrows. Even the stars that usually ornamented the twinkling sky were nowhere to be seen, as if shrinking from the horrors that were unfolding below them.

There was movement inside of the castle, inhabited by some 300 people, but curiously, it was not one of alarm, nor of urgency. Some shuffled about aimlessly by their lonesome, their eyes glazed over and their faces void of expression. Families and loved ones were huddled in corners, their eyes squeezed shut as they muttered last-minute prayers under their breaths. Others were locked in an embrace, whispering words of comfort to their pale-faced companions.

They were cold, numb, and frightened, but there was a haunting sense of peace in the air, for most had resigned to their irreversible fates. They had only mere minutes, perhaps even seconds, to make the life-changing decision looming over them. Were they going to renounce their beliefs and everything that they stood for, or were they willing to become martyrs of what they trusted to be the one true faith?

As these wretched souls awaited their impending doom, however, a band of 3 or 4 elders, accompanied by a local guide, silently headed for the ramparts in the rear of the castle. Cloaked in scratchy woolen blankets, the men pussyfooted to the sturdiest parapet, knotted some sheets around the merlon, and braving the height, rappelled down the side of the wall. They then scampered over to the nearby promontory, and using their sheets, shimmied down to the Lasset gorge.

Not long after they hit the ground, a group of mysterious, similarly cloaked men, faces concealed in their hoods, emerged from the shadows. These were common vassals from the nearby Canton of Sabarthès, who claimed to be the "Sons of the Moon," more precisely, of the moon goddess, Belissena. Though not a word was exchanged between them, each party knew what was expected of them.

With the tick of the proverbial clock ringing in their ears, one of the elders fished out a parcel tucked inside of his cloak, and handed it over to the vassals. And with not a second to spare, the parties parted ways, away from the stampede of soldiers descending to the gorge. The vassals, the new guarders of this priceless treasure, scuttled back into the shadows. The elders, on the other hand, scaled the cliff side and ducked into one of the hundreds of caves in Sabarthès, never to be seen again.

These elders, along with the rest of the unfortunate souls trapped inside the fortress, were none other than the Cathars, and those soldiers were the underlings of the Roman Catholic Church.

Exactly what this priceless treasure was – as well as its existence – continues to be a matter of debate. Some say it was a green jade bowl that possessed otherworldly powers, or maybe, quite literally, just a chest brimming with gold, silver, jewels, and other glittering valuables. Some claim it was a cryptic manuscript comprising the esoteric teachings and other secrets of the Cathars, one so expertly stowed away that it remains missing. Some are convinced that the treasure was of far more significance, one so significant, in fact, that the search for it is one that still persists to this day.

Others insist that it was the fabled Ark of the Covenant that the Cathars handed to the vassals. This 3,000-year-old Biblical artifact, constructed by the Israelites, was believed to be a splendid wooden case coated in gold and garnished with a pair of gilded angels, containing the original stone slabs of the 10 Commandments. It was by some miracle that the Cathars were able to lug that hefty chest all the way down to the gorge.

Then comes what is by far the most popular theory, which identifies the treasure as the Holy Grail. It is an opinion so widespread that Château de Montségur has unofficially been dubbed the "Holy Grail Castle." The Grail in question, still prevalent in modern pop culture, belonged to Christ during the Last Supper, and it was the same chalice Joseph of Arimathea used to bottle the blood of the crucified Christ. Like the sacred Ark, the Grail is often associated with miracles and other supernatural occurrences, such as the feeding of 4,000 with a dozen loaves of bread, and a sinkhole that consumed a disobedient relative of Josephus (son of Joseph of Arimathea), amongst many others.

Whether or not this treasure exists is up for debate, but the atrocities directed toward the Cathars that very evening, as historical records show, cannot be denied. Of course, this begs the question of why the Catholic Church was so determined to annihilate them.

Since most, if not all the Cathar texts were torn to shreds by the Church, their origins can only be left up to speculation. One of the lesser-known etiological myths revolves around Jesus and alleged reformed prostitute, Mary Magdalene, who is oftentimes depicted with an alabaster jar for having famously bathed the feet of Christ with Nardus oil. Following the death and resurrection of Christ, the 12 apostles scattered themselves in all directions to faraway lands, traveling as far as what is now modern day Turkey and India. In the year 44, Mary Magdalene herself was charged with conspiracy against the Roman sovereigns and shunned from her homeland. The road ahead was daunting, but Mary's resilient spirit remained unshaken.

As the Gospel tells it, it was Mary who instilled in the disciples the boundless courage needed to complete their mission. The disciples asked, "How shall we go to the Gentiles and preach the Gospel of the Kingdom of the Son of Man? If they did not spare Him, how will they spare us?" Without missing a beat, Mary sprung up to her feet and commanded her brethren, "Do not week and do not grieve, nor be irresolute, for His grace will be entirely with you, and will protect you."

The legend continues with an unmarked, shoddily made ship sans sails and oars drifting towards and eventually running aground a shore in southern France. One by one, Mary Magdalene, Mother Mary, and her sister, Mary of Clopas piled out of the ship, followed by Lazarus, Martha, and a servant girl named Sarah. The site of their landing, the capital of the Camargue, is now aptly known as the "*Saintes Maries-de-la-Mer,*" or in English, the "Holy Marys from the Sea." Endowed with the honorable task of spreading the word of the Lord, each one of them started towards, and eventually set up camp in a different region of France.

Catholics suggest that Mary Magdalene wound up in the Roman region of Provence in southeastern France, where she reportedly converted all its inhabitants, including the royal family, to Roman Catholicism in no more than 24 hours. She then retreated to the sacred woods now called the Sainte Baume and found shelter inside a cave in the thick of the forest, where she spent the remaining 3 decades of her life. Subsisting on nothing but the bread of the Holy Eucharist, provided to her every day by visiting angels, Mary spent every waking hour either in deep prayer or meditation. Once she took her last breath, the angels swooped into the cave and removed her body.

In the Cathar version of the tale, Mary Magdalene did not end up in Provence but in historical Rennes-les-Bains in what is now Occitanie in southern France. More importantly, according to the Cathars, Mary was not alone; traveling with her was Christ himself, who never died from the crucifixion. As the story goes, Mary crept into his tomb 40 hours after his "death," and together, the pair were secretly whisked away to France.

The Cathar edition also advocates an age-old conspiracy theory that Jesus and Mary Magdalene were husband and wife. Some say that the pair resided in a humble cottage on a hilltop, while others maintain that they lived right in the heart of the community, preferring to live close to those whose hearts they aimed to touch. Rumor has it that some of the townspeople had even chanced upon them in the marketplace and other parts of town, with a few of them swearing that they had also made small talk with them.

Evidently, the pair did not merely adopt the title of husband and wife to fool the townspeople regarding their true identities. The Cathars asserted they then became parents to at least 3 children, two sons and a daughter. The pair lived simply and piously in their cozy cottage until they received word of the townspeople's growing suspicions and interest in their pasts.

It was then that the couple chose to split up. Mary brought with her one of their sons and made the trek up north to what would become Languedoc (the County of Toulose). Joseph of Arimathea was summoned to collect their other son, after which he was dispatched to England. Lastly, Jesus, along with their only daughter, opted to relocate to a more remote residence in the countryside of Rennes-le-Château.

When the hallowed children came of age, they were instructed to go out into the town and preach to the locals the revised doctrine, which gradually evolved and branched out into an array of religious sects and organizations, such as the Essenes, the Knights Templar, and the Cathars. The sons also spawned the bloodlines of the later ruling Arthurian and Merovingian kings in their respective regions. As such, those who propagate these stories say it was the family tree, authentic records, and other proof pertaining to the "perpetuation of the Jesus bloodline" bequeathed to the Cathars that the priests entrusted to the vassals for safekeeping.

While these myths are certainly intriguing, the majority of historians believe that Catharism most likely stemmed from millennia-old Gnostic religions from the East centered on "Dualism." As Bishop Walter Mapp, author of *De Nugis Curialium* ("Trifles of Courtiers"), put it, "Everywhere among Christians [the Cathars] have lain hidden since the time of the Lord's Passion, straying in error."

But even the concept of Dualism itself transcends the birth of Christian Gnosticism, said to be founded by Valentinus of Carthage in the 2nd century CE. The "radical opposition of spirit and matter, good and evil, male and female," as English historian Steven Runciman explains, is "as old as mankind." For instance, there are the harmoniously contrary, yet parallel forces of the yin and yang in Taoism, which bears no link to Christian Gnosticism. The phenomena of good and evil, as well as the conflicting idea of a benevolent God and the evils of material existence, have also been tackled by a host of ancient philosophers, such as the Greek Stoics, Hermetic thinkers, and Jewish scholars from Alexandrian times.

Chroniclers have now concluded that it was from the religion and beliefs of the Bogomils in the Balkans that Catharism descended. The Bogomils were inspired by the Paulicians of Armenia, the latter especially prominent in ancient Armenia between the mid-7th century to late 9th century CE.

The Gnostic Paulicians, in turn, borrowed much of their creed from Manichaeism. Manichaeism, the brainchild of a Persian aristocrat known only as "Mani," was instituted sometime in the 3rd century. The Babylonian sect hosted a distinctive bilateral hierarchical system composed of the Elect, which was a body of high-ranking spiritual leaders selected by the clan, and Hearers, the stock members of the group. The belief system of the Manichee, which guaranteed salvation through the spiritual knowledge passed down by Mani, was an amalgam of Gnostic Christianity, Zoroastrianism, Taoism, and a slew of other mystical theologies, its multifaceted character attracting both admirers and critics.

According to its designer, there are two "natures" that have ruled the earth since the beginning of time – light and darkness. On the one hand, the kingdom of light is marked by serenity and peace of mind, whereas the domain of darkness is in endless war with itself. The creation of the universe, as the designer asserted, was a product of these clashing elements.

Given that stiff discipline was among the core values of the Manichee, members were expected to abstain from swearing, and they were to be strict vegetarians. Their equal treatment of women, which was highly uncustomary at the time, was another norm shattered by the clan. Women, too, could be appointed as members of the Elect.

The Paulicians, another dualist sect, also promoted the belief of two primary forces: good and evil. As the material world was believed to have been a consequence engendered by evil, the Paulicians pledged to distance themselves from all material and carnal pleasures, and shed all vices. Thus, all members swore off meat and alcohol, and vowed to live a life of celibacy.

Much of the information about the Bogomils that exists today is potentially skewed, for the bulk had been gathered by their opponents, i.e., Christian Churches. It is believed that Bogolism came to the fore in the Balkans (now Bulgaria) in the middle of the 10th century, bred by the sect's creator, a priest named Bogomil. The *Interrogatio Iohanni*, the only Bogomil literature known to have survived, preaches a belief system closely aligned with Manichean and Paulician principles in terms of asceticism and dualism.

Contrary to the aforementioned persuasions, the Bogomil belief system relied heavily on Christian themes. Bogomil intended for them to hark back to the earliest, and therefore "purest" form of Christianity, before the rise of what they deemed the increasingly tyrannical Roman Catholic Church. Members were educated about the Gnostic notion of Docetism, which saw Christ as solely a celestial being; this meant that Christ never physically existed, and that his trials and sufferings on earth may have been allegorical. The world, the Bogomils believed, was not an invention of the "God of Light," but His rival, the wicked "Abrahamic God." They rejected crosses and crucifixes alike, and preferred to conduct their rites amidst nature.

It was in the early 1000s that Bogomilism spread to the Byzantine lands, where they grew and soon blossomed. They would have an exceptionally notable presence in Constantinople; in fact, by the end of the century, this "heretical" cult had become so regionally predominant that local leaders, threatened by their influence and proliferation, authorized a brutal campaign against them, a tactic employed by various leaders throughout history. In the year 1118, a ring of Bogomil clerics were rounded up, found guilty at trial for the crime of heresy, and sentenced to death by Emperor Alexius I Comnenus. Among those executed was Basil the Physician, head of the Bogomils.

A contemporary portrait of the Byzantine emperor

In spite of the marked resistance against them, Bogomilism continued to flourish, even extending their reach to Serbia and Bosnia before it was flushed out by Islam following the fall of Constantinople in the 15th century.

Bogomilism made its way to northern Italy by immigrant charcoal burners and other societal outcasts. Through word of mouth, it was then peddled by traveling merchants and Gnostic preachers to civilians in neighboring and distant Italian villages. Their operations naturally shifted to southern France, brought to the region by an unnamed Italian woman, and later, to the villages in northern Spain.

The Bogomil movement was greeted with unexpected warmth and met with surprising success in France. Their fruitfulness was such that more and more converted Bogomils began to discuss and dissect its constitution, which gave way to the advent of an allied, but separate school of thought. It was then that a new denomination, which came to be known as "Catharism," was established. Though the Bogomils and Cathars often held different and sometimes outright contradictory opinions on certain doctrines, the relationship between the sister sects was an amicable one.

As opposed to the other dualist religions, the muse behind the name of the Cathars has not yet been determined. Some say that the name was directly lifted off an older, but then extinct (or perhaps the true predecessor of) sect called the "Cathari," derived from the Greek word "katharoi," which translates into "the pure ones." In the book of St. John Damascene, *On Heresies,* he makes a reference to the sect: "They absolutely reject those who marry a second time, and reject the possibility of penance [that is, forgiveness of sins after baptism]."

The Ecumenical Council of Nicae, which convened in 325 CE, makes another direct mention of this controversial sect in Canon 8: "...if those called "Cathari" come over [to the faith], let them first make profession that they are willing to communicate [share full communion] with the twice-married, and grant pardon to those who have lapsed..."

Allusions to the new-age French Cathars in literature were first made in 1143. A new brand of heresy had been introduced to France by foreign sacrilegious renegades, warned author Everwinus of Steinfeld, who pushed wildly unorthodox theories from Greece that distorted unquestionable Catholic principles. But it was only 22 years later that Eckbert von Schönau mentioned them by their designation, the "Cathars," and elaborated on their dualist beliefs.

The first known complaint lodged against the Cathars by a "concerned" layman was filed in 1177. In a letter addressed to a Cistercian abbot, Count Raymond of Toulouse seeks advice on how best to handle the irreverent "two-principled" heretics that had been running amok in his city. As a result of Raymond's report, a number of accused Cathars were interrogated and duly punished.

By then, the war against the heretics in these parts was nothing new. Toulouse, along with the other localities between the Rhone and the Pyrenees, had been rife with tensions between the Catholic Church and the so-called heretics for hundreds of years. Gnostic sects that labeled Jesus as a mortal prophet and challenged his divinity, such as the Manichee, Bogomils, and Cathars, aroused the most contempt from the Catholic Church, and were among the first names on the establishment's blacklist.

From northern Italy and southern France, Catharism spread to the north of the kingdom. When the strongholds erected there began to flourish in the mid-1100s, the movement traveled further north to the Rhineland cities, gaining remarkable traction in Cologne. But it was in Languedoc that the Cathars truly found their footing, considered by many to be one of the first nerve centers of the community. Indeed, their operations there were so productive that by the end of the 1100s, a majority of the formerly Catholic citizens had converted to Catharism.

Leo Freeman's map of the spread of the sect

Though this new variety of Catharism remained absent from literature until halfway into the 12th century, its members and their ancestors had already endured grievous injustices and abuse at the hands of the Catholic Church for at least more than a century beforehand. Between the years of 1018 and 1028, suspected Cathars, lumped together with the local Manichee by ignorant Church authorities in Aquitaine and Toulouse, became subject to extreme scrutiny. On the 28th of December, 1022, the Feast of the Holy Innocents, 13 Cathar/Manichee elders were arrested in Orléans and condemned to death for their unconventional views on marriage and idolatry, amongst other beliefs. Many incongruous and unfounded yet accepted rumors about the cult's practices, which included members partaking in devil worship, orgies, excessive boozing, and other debauchery, solidified the verdict.

In medieval Europe, one's style of execution was dictated by their crime. Thieves, for example, were sent to the gallows. Adulterers and prostitutes were punished in biblical fashion, and stoned to death for their sins. Those who murdered children were impaled by stakes, their corpses later displayed to the public like trophies. Counterfeiters and con artists were thrown into a vat of bubbling oil and boiled to death. Assassins found guilty of regicide were drawn and quartered.

Death by fire, as it turns out, was a dreadful punishment made exclusive to the heretics. While clearly a needlessly excruciating and traumatic means of execution, it was marketed by the Church as a way to reverse the evil in these "corrupt" souls, as well as to prevent their depravity from infecting the good Christian public. Only by fire, declared Church authorities, could the "smallest trace of sin...and evil" in the ungodly dissenters be thoroughly eliminated. Even the bodies of those who had died of natural and other causes but were posthumously proclaimed as heretics were exhumed and cremated. What's more, the incineration of the heretics' corpses ensured that they would never find the eternal salvation promised to obedient, God-fearing Catholics, for a proper burial was required for resurrection.

The Church leaders at Orléans were set on making an example out of the audacious dissenters. One by one, the shackled prisoners limped in single file to their site of execution as a mob of jeering bystanders pelted them with rotten fruit. Even the queen herself, Constance of Arles, took part in the riotous behavior, ramming her staff into the eye of a passing Cathar named Stephanus. The condemned were marched into a menacing wooden building at the end of the road. All doors, windows, and possible exits were then sealed shut, and the entire building was set ablaze. An excerpt from R. I. Moore, author of *The War On Heresy: Faith and Power in Medieval Europe*, paints a chilling picture of the events: "[W]hen the flames began to burn them savagely, they cried out as loudly as they could from the middle of the fire that they had been terribly deceived by the trickery of the devil, that the views they had recently held of God and Lord of All were bad, and that as punishment for their blasphemy against Him, they would endure much torment in this world, and more in that to come..." The cries of the roasting victims were so distressing that a few rushed forth in a futile effort to extinguish the roaring flames, until they finally accepted that like all the doors and windows on the burning structure, their fates were sealed.

The horrendous events of the 28th of December provided a macabre milestone in European Christian history, for they were supposedly the first burnings of heretics since the 500s. As it turned out, the worst was yet to come.

Creed and Convictions

"But we impart a secret and hidden wisdom of God, which God decreed before the ages for our glory." – 1 Corinthians 2:7

In order to better understand the tempestuous relationship between the Cathars and the Catholics, it is best to analyze the former's nonconformist belief system.

For starters, not only did the Cathars argue that their belief system predated that of the Roman Catholic Church, they maintained that they were "good Christians," which their rivals saw as not just an implication, but proof of the Cathars' supercilious and profane character. Likewise, the Cathars seemed to make no attempts at masking their distrust and loathing of the Catholic Church, which they thought had consciously strayed from the customs and practices of the "Early Church" and generated a conniving and iniquitous system that indulged only the needs and wants of those at the top of the pyramid.

To the Cathars, traditionally classified as Christian Dualists, the "Good God" created, and as such, presides over all that is pure and intangible, meaning all souls – earthly and otherwise – light, love, kindness, and so on. The human race consists of ageless, recycled souls, or as the Cathars called them, "divine sparks." Humans, they claim, are no more than "sparks" or "angels" trapped in vessels of flesh. There were some who believed that the stars they saw strewn across the night skies were other "divine sparks" in heaven, watching over the flock on Earth.

The malevolent God, or simply, "Bad God," the creator of the universe and all the evil inside of it, ruled over these domains. It was he who had hatched the plan to abduct these divine sparks from Heaven, and confine them in fleshly bodies, each made to carry out the agonizing sentence of life in this wicked world. To further frustrate the attempts of the divine sparks to return to the realm of the benevolent God, His counterpart implanted the sin of lust into each one of them, encouraging the procreation of more fleshly prison cells.

Bearing this in mind, the Cathars, like their many forerunners, championed constant prayer and abstinence from all earthly desires, which they believed are the only ways to conquer the diabolic plans of the malevolent God. Even so, piousness and religious restraint are not enough to stave off the evil God; one must possess the strength to withstand external "tortures," such as natural disasters, sickness, famine, and war, not to mention a learned immunity to other temptations presented to them by their peers.

The Cathars' creation myth is summed up in the following excerpt, borrowed from the *Interrogatio Johannis* ("The Questions of John"), believed to be one of their only surviving texts: "And still I, John, questioned the Lord, saying, 'Lord, how did man have spiritual origin in a carnal body?' And the Lord said to me: 'By their fall, spirits of heaven entered the female body of clay, and took on flesh from the lusts of the flesh, and took on [spirit at the same time]...Spirit is born of spirit, and flesh of flesh; and thus, the reign of [the Bad God] ceases not in this world..."

Operating under this logic, the Cathars vocally opposed and detached themselves from the Old Testament, selecting only the second half of the holy book – in particular, the Gospel of John – as their Bible. The Old Testament, they believed, was an undeserved tribute to the malevolent deity. They could not comprehend how one was to bow down before such a cruel and vengeful god, the destroyer of Sodom and Gomorrah and the orchestrator of the terrible flood, who tested his subjects in sadistic fashion; for instance, Abraham, asked to sacrifice his son to God in a show of loyalty. They even went so far as to preach that all patriarchal figures found in the first half of the Bible were "demons" and the sycophantic stooges of the evil God, the greatest of them all being John the Baptist. It was for these reasons that they unequivocally rejected the Old Testament, barring the Ten Commandments.

The antithetical perspectives on Jesus and the Blessed Virgin Mary also led to arguments between the rival Christian faiths. They refuted the virgin birth, stating it was impossible for any mortal to harbor such powers. Instead, Christ, they said, was conceived naturally by Joseph and Mary, and was only "adopted" as God's son following his baptism. In the same breath, they dismissed the idea of the Holy Trinity, for they saw Jesus as his own separate entity, brushing it off as a concept fabricated by the Catholic Church.

While the product of a natural conception and birth, the Cathars' somewhat convoluted delineation of Christ clarifies that he was never mortal, for everything sheltered by skin and muscle is tainted by impurity and could only have been contrived by the malevolent God. Rather, Christ was a spectral being that lived among humankind and endeavored to show them the light of the Good God. This being the case, it was deduced that Christ had never died on the cross, and more importantly, he was never resurrected from the dead, for in doing so, one would require an actual, physical body.

While they were non-believers in the concept of resurrection, the Cathars subscribed to the idea of reincarnation. Upon death, one's soul floats out of one's body, and immediately enters an empty "lodging of clay," which came in seemingly boundless forms, ranging from the embryo in a mother's womb to the slimy egg of a fruit fly. Only those who have lived lives that met or exceeded the standards of the benevolent God were granted permission to return to the Divine Kingdom. Those who neglected or abandoned the path of righteousness were cursed to this perpetual "cycle of rebirth" in this Good-godforsaken planet until they finally decided to alter their lifestyles.

There is an amusing story about a Cathar elder in the usually dismal Inquisition records kept by the Catholic Church regarding this theme. To the annoyance of his guards and interrogators, the elder, a babbling fount of chitchat and never-ending tales, often deflected the line of questioning with anecdotes about one of his past lives as a merry horse. The elder was quoted as saying, "When I was a horse, one night I lost my shoe between 2 stones, and I went on unshod the whole night."

Eberwin von Helfenstein, the Prior of the Premonstratensian Monastery in Steinfeld, Germany, inserts an official statement allegedly issued by the Cathars in a letter to St. Bernard of Clairvaux in 1143, essentially a self-assessment conducted by the persecuted group: "Of themselves they say: 'We are the poor of Christ, who have no fixed abode and flee from city to city like sheep amidst wolves, are persecuted as were the apostles and the martyrs, despite the fact that we lead a most strict and holy life...We undergo this because we are not of this world...We and our fathers, of apostolic descent, have continued in the Grace of God and shall so remain to the end of time..."

The emotive constituents of their belief system allowed the Cathars to justify their many customs. As sexual intercourse, even and especially for the purpose of recreation, yielded more and more "vessels of clay" for the use of the malevolent God, the act, along with marriage itself, was prohibited. Some Cathars, however, understood sex as a natural human desire, and while they still advocated abstinence from marriage, which they considered a "worthless" institution, and procreational sex, they tolerated recreational intercourse, and supported birth control. As the widely-circulated medieval colloquialism goes, "Si non caste tamen caute," or in English, "If not chastely, at least cautiously."

Needless to say, contraceptives at the time, which included the consumption of pomegranates, were in vain, and recreational sex was accordingly still riddled with risk in the Cathars' eyes. On the other end of the spectrum, the Catholics, strictly pro-life, blasted the use of contraceptives. As it so happens, contraception was so reviled by the Church that the act warranted a charge in itself. A 14th century file from the Inquisition archives profiles a French Cathar woman, Beatrice de Planissolles, who was found guilty of the act, along with her unnamed lover, a Catholic priest from Montaillou.

It was in humanity's best interest, the Cathars believed, to remove themselves from all things material, namely anything that brought one any level of pleasure, no matter how negligible. Not unlike their sister sects, the Cathars voiced their disapproval on the ingestion of all animals and animal products, for apart from the taste of their sinfully delicious meat, in doing so, one was eating a fellow divine spark. Interestingly enough, some Cathars were pescatarians, for they believed fish to be soulless creatures, and as such, perfectly fit for consumption.

The Cathars distanced themselves from all tangible material objects, for they are crafted by mankind, derivatives of the malevolent deity. On top of the obvious – that is, money, jewelry, expensive clothing, and so forth – the bread of the Eucharist taken by the Catholics, as well as all crosses, crucifixes, statues, and buildings depicting or dedicated to God, Christ, and other biblical figures, were anything but worthy of veneration. The Christian cross was, to them, by far the most puzzling of all the listed items, for this was to them a torture device. Anyone who worshiped such idols and observed such perversions of God's word were undoubtedly currying favor with the wrong God.

The Catholic Church, whom the Cathars nicknamed the "Church of Wolves," was guiltiest of all when it came to the sin of materialism. The Catholic hierarchy, they claimed, stank of corruption. The Pope, unjustly vested with authority that was comparable to, if not greater than the monarchs of the time, was the wealthiest man in the whole of the continent. Below him on the totem pole were the cardinals, bishops, and priests, who were often seen strutting about in flamboyant, costly robes, and chastised for their luxurious lifestyles, filled with fabulous feasts, opulent homes, and even bevies of women.

Worse yet, they insisted, the Catholic Church was running an intricate and inextricable, but to their credit, well-guarded scam on well-meaning, but clueless Christian folk. The Cathars were not shy about pointing out what they saw as illogical flaws and discrepancies between the Church's teachings and that of the benevolent God's. They equated the "holy water" peddled by the Church, for one, with river water, and the Holy Eucharist with store-bought bread. They not only questioned the instruments of the Church's way of baptism, they denounced their shoving the sacrament down the throats of infant and children, for they believed that only at the age of 18 could one decide whether or not they wanted to commit themselves to God.

Among the most disgraceful of the Church's crimes was its supposed exploitation of followers, both rich and poor. Besides the substantial tithes imposed on the public – which saw every citizen coughing up 10% of their annual incomes, lest they be excommunicated by their priests and bishops – the Church encouraged donations from affluent patrons, which were used to fund top officials' lavish lifestyles. The Cathars also despised the Catholic Church's hawking of burial plots, advertised as one of the only tickets to Heaven. This was another despicable way of preying on the poor, as many found themselves suffocating under the weight of their mounting debts, all for a coveted slot in paradise.

Moreover, the Cathars strove to destroy the credibility of the Catholic priests. As these priests did not abide by the laws of the "Early Church" and were thus terrible sinners themselves, they were not certified to hear confessions, much less forgive them, nor did they have the power to heal the sick through their meaningless oil.

The Cathars attributed much of the Catholics' faults to their pecking order. This being so, the Cathars had no such system, nor did they have a priesthood. There were only two classes of membership within the Cathar order – the credentes, a term given to a standard practitioner of the faith, as well as an inner circle of elites the first Cathars called the "boni homines," or "good men." Later generations referred to them as the "parfait," or the "perfecti" – in English, either "Cathar Perfects," or just the "Elect."

Though only the Perfects were privy to the cult's deepest secrets, and only they who could perform Cathar ceremonies, they made certain never to identify themselves as priests. They were more so a clique of enlightened elders, humble teachers, and faithful missionaries, they claimed, than they were insipid and mindless distributors of a distorted creed. And while the Cathars detested all hierarchies, all entities require some organization to function. The Elect was strengthened with a cabinet of Perfects, all armed with equal power, known as the episcopos. While the word itself meant "bishop," again, they were more akin to the episcopos mentioned in the New Testament, which doubled as "supervisor." Cathar episcopos were each charged with overseeing their own jurisdictions; Inquisition records make references to Cathar bishoprics in Albi, Carcassonne, Cabaret, Toulouse, Montségur, and 5 other localities in southern France alone. Alongside them were two officials called the "filius major," or "Elder Son," and the "filius minor," the "Younger Son," who were entrusted with assisting the episcopos in his management, secretarial work, and other tasks of the like.

The episcopos were also tasked with managing the Cathar communes, including the monasteries, hospitals, and schoolhouses founded by the cult. Apart from these establishments, the Cathars erected various "working craft guilds," mainly related to the arts of weaving, fabric manufacturing, and clothes-making. Not only did these guilds provide clothing for needy Cathars and other impoverished members of the community, the laborious work sharpened the work ethic of the Cathar initiates, also known as the "auditores," their discipline, as well as their ability to follow directions.

As the Cathars prided themselves on being blind to all grades and social castes, anyone, from a "lowly" peasant and blue-collar commoner to the most prestigious member of nobility – and even royalty – could become a perfecti. The only prerequisites for candidacy were an imperishable love for the benevolent God; an unwavering commitment to chastity, charity, simplicity, and other abstinent behavior; and the tenacity to lift the unenlightened from the fogs of misinformation and guide them into the light.

Due to the immense responsibilities incorporated into the job description of the parfait, credentes vying for the position were made to undergo three years training, minimum. They were then inducted into the Elect through a graduation ceremony of sorts known to the Cathars as the "consolamentum," which could only be administered by veteran perfecti. During this pivotal ritual, the gates of Heaven swung open to make way for the Holy Spirit, which traveled down to earth to possess the fleshly body of the perfecti in charge of the ceremony, bestowing upon them the power to provide the divine blessings and authorize the transition. The lack of special vestments, materials, and fanfare in the consolamentum made the Cathar ritual all the more unique.

At times, the consolamentum was also administered to the ill and the injured who believed themselves to be mere seconds away from their last breaths. They hoped that this ritual would cleanse their souls, rendering them worthy enough for entrance into the Pearly Gates. Those who, against all odds, managed to survive their illnesses, were thenceforth regarded as members of the Elect, and were expected to live their lives in such fashion.

Upon the death of an episcopos, they were typically replaced by the Elder Son. The Younger Son was then bumped up into the post of filius major, and the vacant seat filled by another parfait. Apart from providing supplementary support to the episcopos, Sons, which were the Cathars' answers to the Catholics' deacons, were rather hypocritically equipped with the power to hear confessions, a rite they named the "Apareilementum." Parfait, credente, and auditores alike were made to visit their local Sons once a month, and present to them a confession. Depending on the degree of the confession, which ranged from "public" to "solemn," and everything in between, the Sons prescribed to the sinners different levels of atonement that best suited them. "Lighter" sins were mostly met with instructions of prayer and meditation, whereas fasting, prolonged genuflections, and other stricter penances were dispensed to those who had committed "grave" sins.

Contrary to the assumptions of the non-Cathar public, the credentes, though followers of the faith, were urged, but not required to adhere to the hard-line routine and austere lifestyle of a parfait. As a matter of fact, most of the credentes were married, some even bearing children of their own, dined on meat and animal products, and enlisted in wars. And while some – not unlike last-minute Christians and others who made pleas for salvation on their death beds – waited until the last grains of sand wheezed through the narrow neck of their hourglasses before requesting redemption, the majority made it a point to follow set worshiping customs. In addition to upholding the Ten Commandments, the Cathar credentes celebrated Lent three times a year, and semi-fasted three times – most commonly Mondays, Wednesdays, and Fridays – weekly, sticking only to a diet of bland bread and water.

Though the credentes were uninitiated in the innermost secrets of the cult, most of which have since vanished in the vortex of time, all Cathars were taught a special greeting, which was also used at the beginning of the consolamentum. Firstly, the Cathar dropped to their knees, and with interlocked fingers, proceeded to bow thrice, their foreheads kissing the ground each time. Upon each bow, the Cathar recited: "Bless me, Lord; pray for me," before rising off the ground.

During the consolamentum, the Cathar was made to remain on their knees, and delivered the following phrase to the perfecti: "Lead us to our rightful end." To this, the perfecti replied, "God bless you...In our prayers, we ask from God to make a good Christian out of you, and lead you to your rightful end."

The following incantation was also often found in daily Cathar prayers: "Benedicite, Benedicite, Domine Deus, Pater bonorum spirituum, adjuva nos in ommibus quae facere voluerimus." ("Bless us, bless us, O, Lord God, the Father of the spirits of good men, and help us in all that we wish to do").

Another major factor that set the Cathars apart from the Catholic Church was their view on women. Not only were women eligible for a seat in the core crew of elites, some Cathar "bishoprics" were at one time, made up almost entirely of women. Cathar women were such a significant presence in the Cathar community that the ratio of male to female Cathar traitors was close to parallel. One of these turncoats was a Cathar identified only as "Marquese," the wife of Frenchman Bertrand de Prouille. Marquese, the descendant of a long line of Cathars, is said to have served as a spy for the Inquisitors, providing to them intel accumulated from worship meetings and gatherings on 3 separate occasions.

According to Cathar theology, all souls and angels, like their benevolent God, were genderless, and flitted from one body to the other, regardless of sex or form. This, they believed, was why all men and women were equal in intelligence, competence, and capability. Based on this rationale, not only could men and women be admitted into the cult, both male and female Cathar Perfects were deployed to spread the word of the Good God. These *perfecti* were known to travel in pairs and expected to complete their assigned circuits. While the divine sparks were asexual beings, the vessels of clay they inhabited were not, so, these pairs consisted of 2 *parfait* of the same gender.

All Cathars were also technically born with the right to perform "baptisms" (if trained to do so). Even so, this isn't to say that there was absolutely no sexism in the cult; male *parfait* were still most commonly selected to head the *consolamentum* if available, even in some Elects primarily staffed with women.

As strong as their presence was, Cathar women, unsurprisingly, were not always taken seriously. When Esclarmonde de Foix, among the most respected *parfait* in the Cathar community, took the podium during a debate with Dominic Guzman (now better known as "Saint Dominic"), she was immediately reduced to the laughing stock of the council. As told by a witness, the Dominicans, who refused to listen to a woman speak about such consequential matters, attempted to sweep her offstage with their insults, one of them booming: "Go [back] to your spinning, Madame – this debate is no place for you!" To the dismay of the Dominicans, not only did Esclarmonde power through despite the pressure, it was she who had the last laugh, for the Cathars, largely to her contributions, won the debate.

Councils, Synods, and Portentous Preludes

"Frenchmen and clergymen are praised for the evil they make, because they succeed in it." – Peire Cardenal, 1180-1278

A medieval depiction of Peire Cardenal

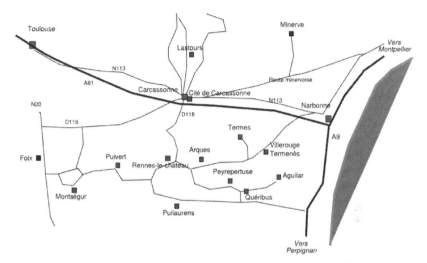

A map of the network of Cathar castles (in blue) across southern France

Medieval France was nowhere close to the 643,800 square kilometers of verdant, strikingly diverse terrain now under the modern state's dominion. Quite the opposite, it was home to a farrago of kingdoms, dukedoms, fiefdoms, and counties, with the disorder heightened by the tangled alliances and divided loyalties of the local governments.

The political turmoil was particularly acute in the Languedoc region. Portions of this colorful, Occitan-speaking district were fiefs that belonged to the Holy Roman Empire, much of it governed by the Catholic Church. Some saluted the French Crown; some paid obeisance to the Aragonese monarchs. Others chose to retain their independence, resisting all the attempts by foreign sovereigns to intervene in their territories. The Counts that chaired Toulouse, a vassal state of the Kingdom of Aragon, were among the most influential and esteemed men in all of Languedoc, for it was they who possessed the richest, and most sizable stretches of land in the region.

Notwithstanding the tricky patchwork of conflicting allegiances in these parts, the inhabitants of Languedoc lived in relative harmony. This was, in large part, thanks to the out-of-character, but ultimately beneficial religious tolerance exhibited by the local leaders – excluding those employed by the Catholic Church – who welcomed immigrants and allowed its burgeoning populaces to embrace and practice whatever faith they so fancied. Smaller governments that took notice of the appreciable upswing in the overall economy of these open-minded territories soon followed suit.

The ineptitude and steadily rising misconduct and dishonesty among the Catholic communities in Languedoc only fueled the multiplication of the dissenters in the area, the most prominent of them being the Cathars. The faith of the people – including the governors of these liberal districts, and even those under the jurisdiction of the Holy Roman Empire – in the Church was fast waning. A litany of complaints directed against the clergy in southern France, branded as indolent, vindictive, and hopelessly unlettered by the progressively growing population of

Languedocian Cathars, was not only threatening to, but succeeding in dismantling the Catholic presence there. Even Pope Innocent III himself would later express his disappointment with his southern French clergy, bitterly likening the priests in Narbonne to "dumb dogs who can no longer bark."

As the Church continued to stumble downhill from the peak of grace, the Cathars pounced on the opportunity to resume their expansion. Toulouse was among the first in the district that was struck by Cathar fervor. The anomalously "modern" and democratic policies of the Counts of Toulouse, along with their laissez-faire attitude towards all colors of religions, and their rejection of the north's feudal systems made it an instant magnet for Cathars, and served as the perfect kindling that allowed the fire of Catharism to spread across the South.

Though Count Raymond VI of Toulouse publicly identified as a Catholic, he maintained a powerful rapport with the Cathars in his county, for many in his family, loved ones, and cortège belonged to the faith. The non-partisan count, who prioritized qualification over background and creed, filled his cabinet with both Catholics and Cathars, and in another unprecedented move, promoted Jews to some of the highest-ranking posts within his administration. By the end of the 12th century, Toulouse had become the 3rd largest city in the whole of Europe, just behind Venice and Rome, and it was swimming in prosperity and a marvelous miscellany of art and cultures.

Raymond VI's seal

As to be expected, the style of Count Raymond's direction drew much criticism from his counterparts, but this would not have been a problem had it not been for his complicated connections. While most of Toulouse belonged to the Aragonese, Raymond also owned several properties in Provence and southeastern France allotted to him by the Holy Roman Emperor and the Kings of France and England. Consequently, much of Raymond's time was devoted to smoothing out internal differences and preserving some semblance of order within the latticework.

From Toulouse, Catharism spread roughly 50 miles northeast to Albi, situated by the River Tarn. Though the faith found some success in establishing a small base in the quiet commune, their presence was nowhere near the extent the Catholics had believed it to be. For reasons unknown, the Church was so adamant that this was the setting of the Cathar's center of operations that they began to refer to all Cathars as "Albigensians."

From Albi, Catharism wandered into Carcassonne, which lay about 67 miles south of the "Cathar center." The Carcassonnians, who had gone from disgruntled to incandescent at the widespread corruption that ran rampant in their local Catholic churches, swiftly responded to this new strain of Christianity, with many relating to and echoing the cult's vehement resentment of the Catholic Church.

It was becoming increasingly difficult for the Church to ignore the spiking number of heretics in the southern neck of France, which soon earned itself the nickname "Cathar (or Albigensian) Country." They were far more proficient in their powers of persuasion than previously thought; over a span of just a few decades, more than 10% of the citizens in Languedoc were calling themselves Cathars.

The survival of the Catholic Church hinged on a time-worn system consisting of 3 "orders," with each echelon in European society properly defined by their given roles. First came the clergy, tasked with enriching and fostering religious life. The nobility, a body that often intertwined with the Church, spearheaded all the decision-making and execution of wars and other political affairs, oversaw the economy, and were charged with the implementation of the justice system. The commoners were saddled with manual labor and grunt work, mostly pertaining to agriculture, though others scraped by as merchants and small-time business owners. Unfortunately for those on the bottom of the barrel, the likelihood of escaping their grueling lives and mountainous debts was slim to none, obstructed by a skewed tax system that allowed nobles and clergymen to rob them blind.

The meddling Cathars disrupted this feudal system. Owing to the cult's promotion of poverty, along with their unabashed disrespect for and insubordination towards the Catholic Church, more and more of the newly-converted Cathars followed by example. Most alarming to the Catholics was the Cathars' bold refusal to pay their due tithes. Threats of excommunication and banishment, which previously had record success rates, no longer packed the same punch. Many of the Cathars presented with such an ultimatum supposedly hooted in the florid faces of their persecutors, and when banished, simply found refuge in the Cathar base of a neighboring town. Even more unnerving was the close bond the Cathars had developed with their local lords.

The Catholic Church began to pick up on the scent of the Cathars at the break of the 11th century, but it only truly began to pursue them in earnest over a century later. Between the years of 1022 (the same year the Church executed the 13 Cathar *perfecti* in Orléans) and 1163, the Cathars were among the top items on the agenda of 8 different Church councils.

It was during the 1163 Council of Tours, hosted by Pope Alexander III, that the term "Albigensian" was first applied, and it soon became glued to the Cathars. Though the schism within the Church at the time was the most pressing matter at hand, the pope, who insisted upon treating the gathering like any other "general council," made certain to address what he saw as the disease of heresy that was spreading unchecked in the southern country. As it was clear that diplomacy and dialogue alone were not enough to stamp out these heretics, it was time for the Church to put its foot down. An excerpt from "Canon 4: Action Against the [Cathars]," penned by Pope Alexander III, read, "In parts of Toulouse a damnably heresy has recently emerged, which is gradually spreading towards neighboring areas and diffusing like a canker, through to Gascony and other provinces, many of which are already infected...Which, while in the form of a snake hiding inside its coil how much more it creeps secretly, more seriously while the Lord's vineyard those of a simple-mind are destroyed..."

A medieval depiction of Pope Alexander III

The pope called upon all Christian princes to pluck out these dreadful Cathars hiding in plain sight and urged them to humiliate them to the fullest degree by throwing them behind bars and seizing their properties. All clergymen and Christian commoners were to regard the Cathars with the same scorn: "It is declared that...all the priests of the Lord having their abode in those parts to be vigilant, and under the penalty of anathema [excommunication] to prohibit them where they are known to follow this heresy, nor to afford any one of them shelter on their land, or presume to impart protection..."

Plainly put, as these heretics were now outlawed, they were to be frozen out by the community. All business relationships with Cathars were to be severed at once, and likewise, all restaurants, marketplaces, and public establishments were banned from serving these heretics. These harsh sanctions were defended by the pope, who explained that the "source of comfort to mankind might at least force them to see the errors of their lives to return to their sentences." Anyone fraternizing with a Cathar was at high risk of being found guilty by association. The same canon warned, "But if any man should attempt to be in opposition to this, and found to be a participant in this iniquity, they shall be smitten by anathema."

At the Third Lateran Council 16 years later, the anti-Cathar canon was revised to include even more stifling sanctions, and after decades of shrugging off the Catholic Church, the indignant Cathars, now wanted by the Catholic Church, finally responded to the councils with a gathering of their own. In 1167, Cathars and other sympathizing Gnostic Christians from all across the country assembled in St. Felix-de-Caraman, just next to Toulouse, for what became known as the first "Cathar Synod." The event, arranged and anchored by the Cathar *episcopos* of France and Lombardy, and Bogomil *papa* Nicetas from their sister sect in the Balkans, thronged with hundreds of fuming *parfait*. But rather than concede defeat, the iron-willed Cathars chose to stand their ground.

The coronation of Pope Innocent III in 1198 only escalated the tensions to new heights. Initially, it appeared that Pope Innocent III, who wished to avoid war at all costs, would attempt to tackle the Cathar issue with "peaceful" tactics. He sent scores of delegates to Cathar country who encouraged them to relinquish their "sacrilegious" faiths through the power of words. However, when none of these delegates could complete their objectives, Pope Innocent turned to Count Raymond VI. In a strategic move, the pope displayed to Raymond, who had been excommunicated for his continuous dealings with the Cathars, a rare act of clemency and granted him a pardon. Obviously, this pardon was not free - in return, Raymond would have to enact the laws decreed by the papal bull and launch a comprehensive campaign against the Cathars.

Pope Innocent III

Meanwhile, the Cathars, sensing dangers of cataclysmic proportions in their midst, began to make preparations for the incoming crisis. In 1204, Lord Ramon of Perella began a series of repairs and renovations on the 40-year-old ruins of the Montségur Fortress for the Cathar perfects, Raymond de Mirepoix and Raymond Blasco. Though the towering walls of the fortress originally functioned as partitions that allowed the Cathars to worship and carry out their rituals outdoors, as specified by their doctrine, it would soon become the "heart of the resistance movement" as the last of the Cathar strongholds.

Once the Château de Montségur ("Castle on the Safe Hill") was fully reconstructed and secured, the fortress was declared the "domicilium et caput," or "House and Head" of the Cathar Church, as ordered by the parfait, Guilhabert de Castres. It became a safe space for all Cathar refugees, fugitives, and faidit (exiles), near and far. The spacious castle was large enough to accommodate 500 at once, and stocked with barrels upon barrels of grain, corn, and water, as well as other provisions.

In 1207, things began to reach a boiling point. At this stage, describing Languedoc as rocked by bedlam would be an understatement. The nobles of the area were squabbling amongst themselves, embroiled in territorial wars (fought by mercenaries) encouraged by the property-hungry Count of Toulouse, and even the relationship between the liege lord and the Languedocian nobility began to sour. That year, unbeknownst to Count Raymond, a papal representative by the name of Peter of Castelnau arranged a string of meetings with the Catholic Languedocian commanders, persuaded them to cease their domestic battles, and convinced them to direct their campaigns towards the Cathars instead. To Peter's chagrin, swaying the convictions of the count would prove far more difficult, as Raymond flat-out refused. Not only was he outraged by the fickleness of the nobles, which now meant that his territorial ambitions would be further delayed, he considered the persecution of any of his citizens, no matter the creed, a disgrace.

Sadly, Raymond was much more malleable the second time around. It took the reinstatement of his excommunication, followed by the loss of the much-needed support from his nobles, a public whipping in Saint Gilles, and a forced public apology to the clergymen he had wronged, for Raymond to finally cave in to the Catholics' demands. In August of 1207, Raymond grudgingly vowed to purge every last Cathar from his lands.

Persecution

"The Roman Church...[says] that the heretics they persecute are the church of wolves. But this is absurd, for the wolves have always pursued and killed the sheep, and today it would have to be the other way around for the sheep to be so mad as to bite, pursue, and kill the wolves, and for the wolves to be so patient as to let the sheep devour them!" – from the alleged writings of the Cathars

At this point, the pope's patience was wearing thin. Count Raymond was dragging his feet, conjuring up one feeble excuse after another as to why no progress was being made on the Cathar "outbreak" in his domains. And when it became clear that Raymond had no intention of keeping up his end of the bargain, the pope retaliated by serving him with an array of apparent "offenses" against the Catholic Church, which included the crime of sympathizing with the Cathars and the theft of Church property, amongst other transgressions. Shortly thereafter, Count Raymond VI was, once again, cut off by the Church.

In January of 1208, a panicking Raymond quickly requested the presence of Peter of Castelnau in Saint Gilles, and he begged for the papal delegate to plead his case to his superiors on his behalf. Peter agreed to meet with Raymond, and the pair deliberated the matter over the course of the next few days, but it did not take long for these negotiations to turn into heated debates. It was during their last meeting on the 15th of January that matters truly got ugly, so much so that the event ended with a furiously cursing Raymond lunging at Peter in front of more than half a dozen witnesses. Once Raymond had been peeled off of Peter, the livid delegate strode out of the count's chambers and stomped off his estates, determined not to look back. In hindsight, it seemed that Peter might have been better off doing just that, for as fate would have it, the moment he turned down the road by Saint Gilles Abbey, a knife was plunged into his back. He was discovered just a few hours later, but by then, his corpse was already beginning to stiffen.

Though the assailant was never identified, Pope Innocent III was the first to point a finger in Raymond's direction. Luckily for Raymond, due to the lackluster weight of his hearsay-based evidence and unsubstantiated claims, not to mention the absence of witnesses, he was never brought to trial.

That said, the murder of Peter of Castelnau was enough to provoke the already restless pope into waging a full-scale war against the Cathars. On March 10, 1208, the day of Peter's canonization, the pope summoned the Christian Crusaders and unleashed upon them a riveting, albeit long-winded, speech: "Forward then, Christian knights! Forward, courageous recruits of the Christian army! May a pious zeal set you on fire to avenge so great an offense against your God!...The ship of the Church will suffer total shipwreck unless it gets some strong help in this unprecedented storm. This is why...we order you...in the name of Christ, in the face of such peril, we promise the remission of your sins, so that you may thwart such dangers without delay."

The pope urged them to unshackle all inhibitions and shed all restraints when dealing with these heathens: "Be diligent to destroy the heresy by any means God will inspire you to use. With greater assurance than with the Saracens, since they are more dangerous, fight the heretics with a mighty hand, and an outstretched arm...Strip them of their land, so that Catholics may replace the eliminated heretics and serve in God's presence...according to the discipline of your orthodox faith."

Even the pope himself would later admit that there existed no evidence tying Raymond, or any other Cathar, to the cold-blooded murder. Others accused the Catholic Church of choreographing and executing the assassination themselves in a desperate bid to justify violence against the heretics, but they, too, had no concrete evidence.

Whatever the case, the Catholics proceeded with their campaign, and in 1209, the Albigensian Crusade began.

The first Catholic battalion of about 10,000–20,000 strong began their march south from Lyon in early spring of that year. Leading the crusade was Simon de Montfort, an English-French aristocrat and seasoned military general. Assisting him in this momentous campaign were the Counts of Saint-Pol and Nevers, the Seneschal of Anjou, the Duke of Burgundy, and other veteran captains with equally glittering careers.

The party continued to slog through the rough terrain along the River Rhone, heading for Provence, where they were later united with the "Spiritual Adviser" of the Crusade, Arnaud Amalric. This was the same Arnaud Amalric who, when asked how to distinguish between the Cathars and Catholics, reportedly uttered the famous phrase now most commonly associated with the Albigensian Crusade: "Kill them all. The Lord will recognize His own."

The Catholic forces laid siege to Cathar Country with ease, and in late July the Cathars experienced the magnitude of the crusaders' savagery for the first time. On the 21st of that month, Catholic troops descended upon the Langudeocian town of Béziers, which was under the guardianship of Raymond-Roger Trencavel III, the Viscount of Béziers and Carcassonne. Trencavel stepped forward to receive the Catholic generals at once, and when he failed to reach an understanding with them, alerted his uncle, the Count of Toulouse, and petitioned him for help. To Trencavel's consternation, not only did Raymond decline, many of the Count's own soldiers had been integrated into the same Catholic troops stationed at Béziers.

The Catholic generals demanded from Trencavel a list of 222 Cathars – evidently, to fill a quota they had been provided by the Church – but to this, Trencavel refused. The next morning, tens of thousands of Catholic soldiers surrounded the Basilica of St. Mary Magdalene, where 20,000 locals gathered for Mass, bolted it shut, and promptly torched the place. All men, women, and children perished in the flames. When the soldiers later learned that they would not be keeping the plunder from Béziers - it would instead be used to fund the ongoing crusade - the seething soldiers rioted and razed the city to the ground.

A medieval depiction of the pope excommunicating the Cathars and the Catholics massacring them

The Catholic generals proceeded to their next major target, Carcassonne, on the 1st of August, 1209. This Cathar stronghold, overflowing with Cathar refugees who had escaped the crusade up north, was enclosed by 26 armed towers, just above the River Aude, but these defenses soon proved to be no more than glorified fences. The Catholics closed in on the stronghold's most indispensable resource – the River Aude – and succeeded in holding its water supply hostage in less than a week. By the 15th, Carcassone had raised a white flag, and Trencavel was imprisoned in the dungeon of his very own fortress, where he died from dysentery about a month later. Though Carcassonne was spared a bloodbath, all Cathars, dissenters, and sympathizers were ousted from the city, taking with them "nothing but their sins."

Modern pictures of Carcassonne

The Crusaders went on to enjoy an uninterrupted winning streak for the next six years, and though the Cathars managed to muster up the strength and manpower to defend themselves effectively, even reclaiming most of the lands they had been robbed of by 1225, their "victories" were short-lived. Just four years later, Languedoc was absorbed into the French kingdom, and a new type of operation to eliminate the heretics was unveiled in the form of the Inquisition.

Considering the skyrocketing number of bizarre and disturbing rumors that hounded the heretics in the 13th century, it seemed as if the Catholics had created a department solely dedicated to churning out anti-Cathar propaganda. First and foremost, they capitalized on the death of Peter of Castelnau and the gullibility of the grieving followers. When commemorating Peter's death, whom they now hailed as a "martyr," they concluded their poignant accolades with his last words: "May God forgive thee, brother, as I fully forgive thee." It did not matter that there were no witnesses to his death – the Catholics accepted this as fact.

Apart from vilifying the Cathars as callous and heartless murderers, the Catholics used what little they knew about Cathar doctrine, twisting truths to further their agenda. Due to the Cathars' unorthodox views on sex and marriage, they were accused of being chronic masturbators, and engaging in incest, bestiality, and other unthinkable acts. They were branded as sodomites, often using the Cathars' preference to travel in duos of the same gender as proof. The Catholics themselves, including many a pope, were also no strangers to the "crime" of sodomy, but to them, of course, that was neither here nor there.

The year 1231 marked the beginning of the Inquisition against the Cathars in southern France. Three religious judges (titled "commissioners") were to be sent to each parish, and Catharism was to be uprooted. There, they would, as dictated by the Council of Toulouse in 1229, be "specially charged with seeking out the heretics from the cellar to the attic, and denouncing them to the bailiffs."

Bailiffs and interrogates sent by the Inquisitors were then tasked with conducting "interviews" with suspected Cathars. Those deemed guilty were afforded a "grace period" of two days to publicly denounce their heretical faiths and convert to the one "true" version of Christianity. Those who capitulated were met with mercy and released with a warning. That said, these first-time offenders were made to don, "from now on and forever," a pair of bright yellow cross measuring about 10 inches on their chests and collars, as a permanent reminder of the deplorable sin they had committed. As degrading as these distinctive badges of shame – or as the locals called them, "las debanadoras," or "winders" – were, the Cathars made sure to have them pinned onto them at all times, for failure to do so could earn one a second conviction, which meant the death penalty.

Cathars who refused to renounce their faiths were taken to trial, where they were to be tried by two chief Inquisitors, the Lord of the land, and other local court officials. Inquisitors presented to the court the evidence against the accused, which typically came in the form of testimonies, spy reports, and so on, until the Cathar made a full confession. It was then that the Cathar was passed off to state authorities, who settled upon an "appropriate" punishment for the heretic.

Some of the convicted were imprisoned, as instructed by the Catholic Church: "Every heretic whose conversion was not obtained by devotion but by fear of the laws, be detained in a fortress, so that he cannot defile others…" Though sentenced to life in prison, the conditions in these dungeons were so abysmal that many quickly met with death. Conversely, Cathars deemed "unsalvageable," as well as second-time offenders, were fed to the flames. Some were thrust into burning buildings, asphyxiating before the flames devoured their corpses. Others were tethered to stakes and engulfed by the raging bonfire. These methods of execution by fire only became more creative with time. Such methods included the frying of Cathars in drums of sulfur, resin, and oil. On other occasions, the Catholics roasted the heretics alive in ovens or broiled them on gridirons.

A depiction of Cathars being burned at the stake

The Inquisitors' obsession with the Cathars was so frightening that both Cathars and non-Cathars lived in equal fear for their lives. Many were convicted solely on the testimonies of their neighbors, who were often incentivized by their own safety. The lax requirements for these testimonies also gave way to numerous grudge-bearers exacting their revenge on business rivals and enemies. After all, even if their testimonies were disproven, they could be let off the hook by simply stating that they had been innocently misguided by their "zeal for the Faith."

Upon the death of the Cathar, half – and in many cases, all – of his or her property, which was previously to be passed on to their surviving family members, was confiscated by the Church.

Soon, the Church, as suggested by the Dominicans, began to administer postmortem trials. Those found guilty of Catharism were dug up and stripped of their valuables, and their assets were taken from their heirs.

Following the demise of Simon de Montfort in 1218, Pope Honorious III started yet another crusade against the Cathars, and it would result in the Cathars' last stand against the Catholics at Montségur.

Pope Honorious III

The fortress of Montségur, as well as a modest "terraced" village under the northeastern wing of the castle, provided a sanctuary for hundreds of displaced Cathars. Another small concentration of the refugees lay in the outpost on the northern end of the pog, which they christened "Roc de la Tour," or "Tower Rock," as early as 1233. The 150 soldiers – captained by Pierre-Roger Mirepoix – who manned the last Cathar base knew that it was only a matter of time before they would be overpowered by the Catholics, but they were seemingly undaunted and determined to fight to the end.

In the end, the efforts of Lord Ramon of Perella paid off after all, at least somewhat, for it took the Catholics over 8 months to finally outsmart and overcome the Cathars' barriers. In January of 1244, the Catholic troops succeeded in infiltrating and capturing Tower Rock, the lowest level of the fortress. From there, the Catholics continued to make the winding hike up to the main castle. By the end of February, they were close enough for their trebuchets to lob giant boulders and other projectiles at the fortress walls.

The small Cathar army made a few futile attempts at resistance, but predictably, they could not compete with the Catholics who vastly outnumbered them. On the 1st of March, a heavyhearted Mirepoix surrendered the fortress and took part in the negotiations of a ceasefire. In an unusual display of leniency, the Catholics were prepared to grant all Cathars and mercenaries their freedoms, even allowing the latter to keep their arms, so long as they disavowed Catharism and converted to the true faith. The majority of the Cathar, most of them parfait, calmly declined the life-saving offers. Another 26 mercenaries followed in tow, and on the 13th of March, requested the rite of consolamentum from present elders. Three mornings later, a total of 225 Cathars were led down to the southern slopes of the pog, where every last one of them would be burned at the stake.

The Roman Inquisition, launched shortly afterwards, wiped out the last of the Cathars, and by the early 14th century, the Catholic Church declared Catharism extinct. The 1323 burning of Guilhem Belibaste, a perfecti who had been outed by an undercover Catholic while hiding out in Morella, is now widely thought to be the execution of the world's last Cathar.

Online Resources

Other books about the Cathars on Amazon

Bibliography

Mack, G. (2014, March 23). THE CATHAR TREASURE: CRUSADING FOR GOD, SEARCHING FOR ILLUMINATION OR MINING FOR GOLD? Retrieved January 18, 2018, from http://gayemack.com/tag/cathar-myths/

Mack, G. (2013, June 6). THE MEDIEVAL CATHARS-ROME'S RATIONALE FOR ITS BRUTAL INQUISITION. Retrieved January 18, 2018, from http://gayemack.com/the-medieval-cathars-romes-rationale-for-its-brutal-inquisition/

Editors, W. H. (2015, September 3). The Cathar Treasure. Retrieved January 18, 2018, from http://www.worldhistory.biz/middle-ages/24419-the-cathar-treasure.html

Mann, J. (1996). The Legend of the Cathars. Retrieved January 18, 2018, from https://www.bibliotecapleyades.net/mistic/esp_cataros_03.htm

Wynants, E. (1986). The Church's War on the Cathars. Retrieved January 18, 2018, from https://www.bibliotecapleyades.net/mistic/esp_cataros_07.htm

Editors, N. N. (2010, June 6). The Cathars And The Holy Grail. Retrieved January 18, 2018, from https://archaeologynewsnetwork.blogspot.tw/2010/06/cathars-and-holy-grail.html#TpJZzuAPSQe8IMyt.97

Wronski, P. (2002). MONTSEGUR IDENTITIES OF CATHARS EXECUTED ON MARCH 16, 1244. Retrieved January 18, 2018, from http://www.russianbooks.org/montsegur/montsegur5.htm

Cline, A. (2017, November 6). Cathars & Albigenses: What Was Catharism? Retrieved January 18, 2018, from https://www.thoughtco.com/cathars-and-albigenses-249504

McDonald, J. (2017, February 8). Cathars and Cathar Beliefs in the Languedoc Timeline & Chronology of Events. Retrieved January 18, 2018, from http://www.cathar.info/cathar_chronolgy.htm

Editors, H. P. (2018). Albigensian Crusade Facts & Timeline. Retrieved January 18, 2018, from https://historyplex.com/albigensian-crusade-facts-timeline

McDonald, J. (2017, February 8). Cathars and Cathar Beliefs in the Languedoc Cathar Wars or "Albigensian Crusade". Retrieved January 18, 2018, from http://www.cathar.info/cathar_wars.htm

Editors, M. B. (2014, March 12). Mary Magdalene and the Cathars. Retrieved January 18, 2018, from http://www.marymagdalenebooks.com/mary-magdalene-and-the-cathars

Gouzy, M. N. (1997, January 6). An Age of Persecution. Retrieved January 18, 2018, from https://www.bibliotecapleyades.net/mistic/esp_cataros_04.htm#persecution

Editors, W. P. (2015, November 2). The Cathars and Reincarnation. Retrieved January 18, 2018, from https://www.watkinspublishing.com/the-cathars-and-reincarnation/

Editors, W. B. (2016, August 22). The Siege of Montsegur. Retrieved January 18, 2018, from https://writeonthebeach.wordpress.com/2016/08/22/the-siege-of-montsegur/

Editors, G. L. (2012). Cathar Texts and Rituals. Retrieved January 18, 2018, from http://gnosis.org/library/Interrogatio_Johannis.html

McDonald, J. (2017, February 8). Cathar Beliefs. Retrieved January 18, 2018, from http://www.cathar.info/cathar_beliefs.htm

Editors, C. H. (2013). #211: Cathars Recorded as Heretics. Retrieved January 19, 2018, from https://christianhistoryinstitute.org/study/module/cathars

Editors, T. T. (2016). The Cathars. Retrieved January 19, 2018, from https://twelvetribes.org/articles/cathars

Editors, R. L. (2012, February 2). Chateau de Montsegur. Retrieved January 19, 2018, from http://www.renneslechateau.nl/2012/02/02/chateau-de-montsegur/

Lovett, R. A., & Hoffman, S. (2015). Ark of the Covenant. Retrieved January 19, 2018, from https://www.nationalgeographic.com/archaeology-and-history/archaeology/ark-covenant/

Editors, H. C. (2016). HOLY GRAIL. Retrieved January 19, 2018, from http://www.history.com/topics/holy-grail

Beavis, M. A. (2013). Who is Mary Magdalene? Retrieved January 19, 2018, from https://www.baylor.edu/content/services/document.php/199647.pdf

Lavino, A. (2018). Mary Called Magdalene. Retrieved January 19, 2018, from http://www.sacredmysterytours.com/mary-magdalene/#sthash.u49BbAYx.SEch45Lu.dpbs

Daoutt, J. (2015). Mary Magdalene. Retrieved January 19, 2018, from http://www.panoccitania.com/magdalene.html

Marrs, J. (2011). The Pure Ones. Retrieved January 19, 2018, from https://www.bibliotecapleyades.net/mistic/esp_cataros_06.htm

Editors, G. C. (2015). Chapter 55: Sex, Lies, And Fairy Tales. Retrieved January 19, 2018, from http://genesis6conspiracy.com/chapter-55-sex-lies-and-fairy-tales/

McDonald, J. (2017, February 8). Where did Catharism come from ? Retrieved January 19, 2018, from http://www.cathar.info/cathar_origins.htm

Watkins, T. (2007). The Cathars: Their Nature, Origin and Demise. Retrieved January 19, 2018, from http://www.applet-magic.com/cathars.htm

Van Schaik, J. L. (2006, March 7). CATHARS, ALBIGENSIANS, and BOGOMILS. Retrieved January 19, 2018, from http://www.iranicaonline.org/articles/cathars-albigensians-and-bogomils

O'Neill, R. (2013, October 1). Origins of Catharism. Retrieved January 19, 2018, from https://www.tarot.com/tarot/robert-oneill/catharism-and-the-tarot-introduction

Editors, T. (2005, July 15). Cathar. Retrieved January 19, 2018, from http://www.thelemapedia.org/index.php/Cathar

Knight, K. (2017). Albigenses. Retrieved January 19, 2018, from http://www.newadvent.org/cathen/01267e.htm

Merillat, H. C. (1997). Medieval Pure Ones. Retrieved January 19, 2018, from http://gnosis.org/thomasbook/ch12.html

Coppens, P. (2008). THE WAR ON THE CATHARS. Retrieved January 22, 2018, from http://www.gnostic.info/the-war-on-the-cathars/

Costagliola, M. (2015, September 30). Fires in history: the cathar heresy, the inquisition and brulology*. Retrieved January 22, 2018, from https://www.ncbi.nlm.nih.gov/pmc/articles/PMC4883611/

Editors, M. M. (2011). The Cave of Magdalene ....a French experience. Retrieved January 22, 2018, from http://www.marymagdalenewisdom.com/the-cave-of-magdalene/

Graves, D. (2010, April 28). GNOSTICISM. Retrieved January 22, 2018, from https://www.christianity.com/church/church-history/timeline/1-300/gnosticism-11629621.html

Editors, E. T. (2013, December 28). 1022: Medieval Europe's first heresy executions. Retrieved January 22, 2018, from http://www.executedtoday.com/2013/12/28/1022-orleans-heresy/

Editors, A. H. (2015). The Heretics at Orléans. Retrieved January 22, 2018, from https://theamalricianheresy.wordpress.com/the-heretics-at-orleans/

McDonald, J. (2017, February 8). Melhoramentum. Retrieved January 22, 2018, from http://www.cathar.info/cathar_beliefs.htm#melhoramentum

McDonald, J. (2017, February 8). Roman Catholic Propaganda. Retrieved January 22, 2018, from http://www.cathar.info/cathar_catholic.htm#other

Editors, A. W. (2013, February 9). Cathar Perfect. Retrieved January 22, 2018, from http://arcana.wikidot.com/cathar-perfect

Saxon, Y. (2013, February 26). THE LAST CATHAR. Retrieved January 22, 2018, from https://thedailybeagle.net/2013/02/26/the-last-cathar/

Editors, G. L. (2014). Consolamentum (Consolament). Retrieved January 22, 2018, from http://gnosis.org/library/Consolamentum.html

Barber, M. (2016, September 17). Women and Catharism. Retrieved January 22, 2018, from http://www.medievalists.net/2016/09/women-and-catharism/

Editors, L. L. (2016, September 9). Cathar women. Retrieved January 22, 2018, from http://www.languedocliving.com/cathar-women-life-834.html

Wronski, P. (2002). THE CATHAR FAITH: A CRITICAL INTRODUCTION. Retrieved January 22, 2018, from http://www.russianbooks.org/montsegur/montsegur1.htm

Loflin, L. (2012). Who are the Cathers? Retrieved January 22, 2018, from http://www.sullivan-county.com/id2/gnostic_files/cather.htm

Editors, M. (2013, December 2). Birth Control and Abortion in the Middle Ages. Retrieved January 22, 2018, from http://www.medievalists.net/2013/12/birth-control-and-abortion-in-the-middle-ages/

Carr, K. (2017, August 4). Tithes – medieval Church taxes. Retrieved January 22, 2018, from https://quatr.us/medieval/tithes-medieval-church-taxes.htm

Editors, L. F. (2011). Article on the Cathars. Retrieved January 22, 2018, from http://www.languedoc-france.info/articles/a_cathars.htm

Nullens, G. (2013). 1.7 The End of the Cathars. Retrieved January 22, 2018, from https://nullens.org/catholics-heretics-and-heresy/part-1-the-cathars/1-7-the-end-of-the-cathars/#.WmebC6iWZPZ

McDonald, J. (2017, February 8). Inquisition against the Cathars of the Languedoc. Retrieved January 22, 2018, from http://www.cathar.info/cathar_inquisition.htm

Editors, A. F. (2016). What and where is "le Pays Cathare", and who were the Cathars? Retrieved January 22, 2018, from https://about-france.com/tourism/cathar-country.htm

Editors, F. W. (2017). Cathars in France: the cathar religion and the hilltop Languedoc cathar castles. Retrieved January 22, 2018, from http://www.francethisway.com/history/history-cathars.php

Editors, H. H. (2011, November 7). Cathar Heresy – Count Raymond VI of Toulouse. Retrieved January 22, 2018, from http://historytimeshistory.blogspot.tw/2011/11/cathar-heresy-count-raymond-vi-of.html

Mann, J. (2014). The Cathars an Introduction. Retrieved January 22, 2018, from http://www.internationalschooltoulouse.net/y8/term1/cathars/info.htm

Editors, M. F. (2007). Historic Towns: Albi (The Name in Occitan. Clich here to find out more about occitan. Albi). Retrieved January 22, 2018, from http://www.midi-france.info/030402_albi.htm

Delingpole, J. (2017, July). Cathar country, Carcassonne and cassoulet. Retrieved January 22, 2018, from https://www.spectator.co.uk/2017/07/cathar-country-carcassonne-and-cassoulet/

Editors, M. C. (2009). Catharism. Retrieved January 22, 2018, from http://mescladis.free.fr/ANGLAIS/pages%20html/catharism.htm

Editors, C. C. (2013, October 24). Council of Tours 1163. Retrieved January 22, 2018, from http://conclarendon.blogspot.tw/2013/10/council-of-tours-1163.html

Editors, W. W. (2007). Ramon de Perella . Retrieved January 22, 2018, from http://www.wikiwand.com/ca/Ramon_de_Perella

Editors, P. M. (2011, August 7). Papal legate Peter of Castelnau is murder 1208. Retrieved January 23, 2018, from http://professor-moriarty.com/info/fr/thisday/papal-legate-peter-castelnau-murder-1208

Editors, R. R. (2012, January 15). On this day ... the murder that allows Pope Innocent III to launch the Albigensian Crusade. Retrieved January 23, 2018, from https://realrometours.wordpress.com/2012/01/15/on-this-day-the-murder-that-allows-pope-innocent-iii-to-launch-the-albigensian-crusade-2/

Editors, C. O. (2013). Bl. Peter of Castelnau. Retrieved January 23, 2018, from http://www.catholic.org/saints/saint.php?saint_id=5303

Editors, X. G. (2006, November 20). CATHARISM. Retrieved January 23, 2018, from http://www.xenophongroup.com/montjoie/albigens.htm

Editors, C. B. (2015). The Inquisition. Retrieved January 23, 2018, from http://catholicbridge.com/catholic/inquisition.php

Editors, C. C. (2016). The Cathars and The Inquisitors. Retrieved January 23, 2018, from http://cordessurciel.eu/history/cathars/

Editors, E. N. (2016). GRIDIRON. Retrieved January 23, 2018, from https://erenow.com/common/execution-a-guide-to-the-ultimate-penalty/28.html

Editors, R. B. (2011). 4. THE SIEGE OF MONTSEGUR 1243-1244 . Retrieved January 23, 2018, from http://www.russianbooks.org/montsegur/montsegur3.htm

Editors, R. B. (2011). 5. THE FALL OF MONTSEGUR - MARCH 1244 . Retrieved January 23, 2018, from http://www.russianbooks.org/montsegur/montsegur4.htm

Russell, J. B. (1965). *Dissent and Reform in the Early Middle Ages*. University of California Press.

Rahn, O. (2006). *Crusade Against the Grail: The Struggle between the Cathars, the Templars, and the Church of Rome*. Simon and Schuster.

Lacy, N. J. (2010). *Lancelot-Grail: The quest for the Holy Grail*. Boydell & Brewer Ltd.

Vasilev, G. (2007). *Heresy and the English Reformation: Bogomil-Cathar Influence on Wycliffe, Langland, Tyndale and Milton*. McFarland.

De Pélhisson, G. (1974). *Heresy, Crusade and Inquisition in Southern France 1100-1250* (W. L. Wakefield, Trans.). University of California, Berkeley.

Free Books by Charles River Editors

We have brand new titles available for free most days of the week. To see which of our titles are currently free, click on this link.

Discounted Books by Charles River Editors

We have titles at a discount price of just 99 cents everyday. To see which of our titles are currently 99 cents, click on this link.

Made in the USA
Las Vegas, NV
14 December 2025

36384615R00024